SKILLED AND VOCATIONAL TRADES

BECOME AN HVAC TECHNICIAN

by Carla Mooney

BrightPoint Press

San Diego, CA

BrightPoint Press

an imprint of ReferencePoint Press, Inc.
Printed in the United States

For more information, contact:
BrightPoint Press
PO Box 27779
San Diego, CA 92198
www.BrightPointPress.com

LIBRARY OF CONGRESS CATALOGING-IN-PUBLICATION DATA

Name: Mooney, Carla, author.
Title: Become an HVAC technician / by Carla Mooney.
Description: San Diego, CA: ReferencePoint Press, 2027 | Series: Skilled and vocational trades | Includes bibliographical references and index. | Audience: Grades 7–9
Identifiers: ISBN 9781678214623 (hardcover) | ISBN 9781678214630 (eBook)
The complete Library of Congress record is available at www.loc.gov.

CONTENTS

AT A GLANCE

- HVAC technicians work with heating, cooling, and ventilation systems in homes and businesses.

- HVAC workers install, repair, and maintain HVAC systems.

- Trade schools and vocational programs teach students to be HVAC technicians. They even give students opportunities for hands-on practice.

- Some beginners learn to be HVAC technicians through apprenticeships. These programs pair them with expert HVAC professionals.

- Important skills for HVAC technicians include math skills, technical skills, people skills, and problem-solving skills.

- Many HVAC technicians work for HVAC companies. Others are self-employed.
- The number of HVAC technician jobs is expected to grow by about 8 percent from 2024 to 2034.
- HVAC technology continues to evolve. HVAC technicians will need to learn to work with new technology and systems.

KEEPING COOL IN A HEAT WAVE

In July 2025, a heat wave swept through Philadelphia, Pennsylvania. Temperatures soared. The heat wave lasted several days.

The high heat gave dentist David Yarmark a big problem. Yarmark's dental office was unbearably hot. The office's air conditioning system had stopped working. Yarmark was forced to close the office. "It got really hot in here and at the dental office, that's not fun," Yarmark says.[1]

HVAC repair and installation is a multibillion-dollar industry.

Commercial HVAC systems keep customers comfortable.

Yarmark turned to Doug Stiefel for help. Stiefel owns PJ Mac HVAC Service & Repair. HVAC stands for heating, ventilation, and air conditioning. Heating and air conditioning keep buildings at comfortable temperatures. Ventilation controls how much outside air comes inside a building. Stiefel is an experienced HVAC technician. These skilled workers install and repair HVAC systems.

Stiefel arrived at the dental office. He **inspected** the air conditioning system. Stiefel found the problem. The compressor was broken. The compressor is a key part of an air conditioning system. It works like a pump that keeps the cooling process moving. When the compressor breaks, the cooling process stops.

Stiefel replaced the broken part. He got the air conditioning system running again. Yarmark was able to reopen his office. "Being able to get up and running again was wonderful," says Yarmark.[2]

During heat waves, Stiefel gets many calls. People ask him for help. Their homes are too hot. Their air conditioning is not working. Stiefel was very busy during Philadelphia's 2025 heat wave. The hot weather put a lot of stress on air conditioning systems. He says that an air conditioning system might cool enough at lower temperatures, but adds, "When it's [90°F (32°C)] and above, it doesn't work as well."[3]

Stiefel recommends that people get regular **maintenance** for their heating

HVAC units should be inspected at least once a year.

and cooling systems. This can prevent unexpected problems. Before the heat wave, he performed maintenance for a fire station. Stiefel discovered a faulty part. He replaced the part before it became a problem. The fire station stayed cool and comfortable during the heat wave.

Some HVAC systems are built into homes. Others are portable.

HVAC TECHNICIANS

HVAC technicians work with heating, cooling, and ventilation systems in homes and businesses. These skilled workers install new HVAC systems. They also repair broken systems. They make sure heaters keep buildings warm in winter. They ensure air conditioners keep buildings cool in summer.

HVAC workers also clean ventilation systems. This helps improve air quality. They test systems. They make sure systems are safe. They ensure everything works correctly. Their skills help people stay comfortable and healthy indoors.

WHAT DOES AN HVAC TECHNICIAN DO?

HVAC technicians help keep buildings comfortable. HVAC workers service systems that heat, cool, and clean air. They work in homes, schools, businesses, and more. Their work helps people live, learn, and work in safe and comfortable spaces.

HVAC workers also help control humidity in a building. Humidity is how wet or dry the air feels. Air that is too wet can cause mold. Air that is too dry can be uncomfortable.

Businesses should generally be kept between 68°F and 76°F (20°C and 24°C).

HVAC workers adjust heating and cooling systems. They monitor humidity. Their work keeps the air balanced and healthy.

HOW DO HVAC SYSTEMS WORK?

There are many types of heating and cooling systems. But most work in similar ways. Cooling systems work by removing heat from the air. Warming systems work by creating heat.

Air conditioners use a special fluid called refrigerant. When a person turns an air conditioner on, the refrigerant moves through the air conditioner. Pieces inside the air conditioner use pressure to change the liquid into a gas and back again. This changes the temperature of the liquid. When refrigerant turns into a gas, it

Refrigerant isn't used up when it cools air, so it needs to be replaced only if it leaks.

becomes cold. The refrigerant absorbs heat from inside a room. It then transfers that heat outside as it turns back into a liquid. Then the process starts again

Window air conditioners sit in windows. They cool air in those rooms. This gradually changes the temperature of the rest of the building.

HOW DO FORCED AIR COOLING SYSTEMS WORK?

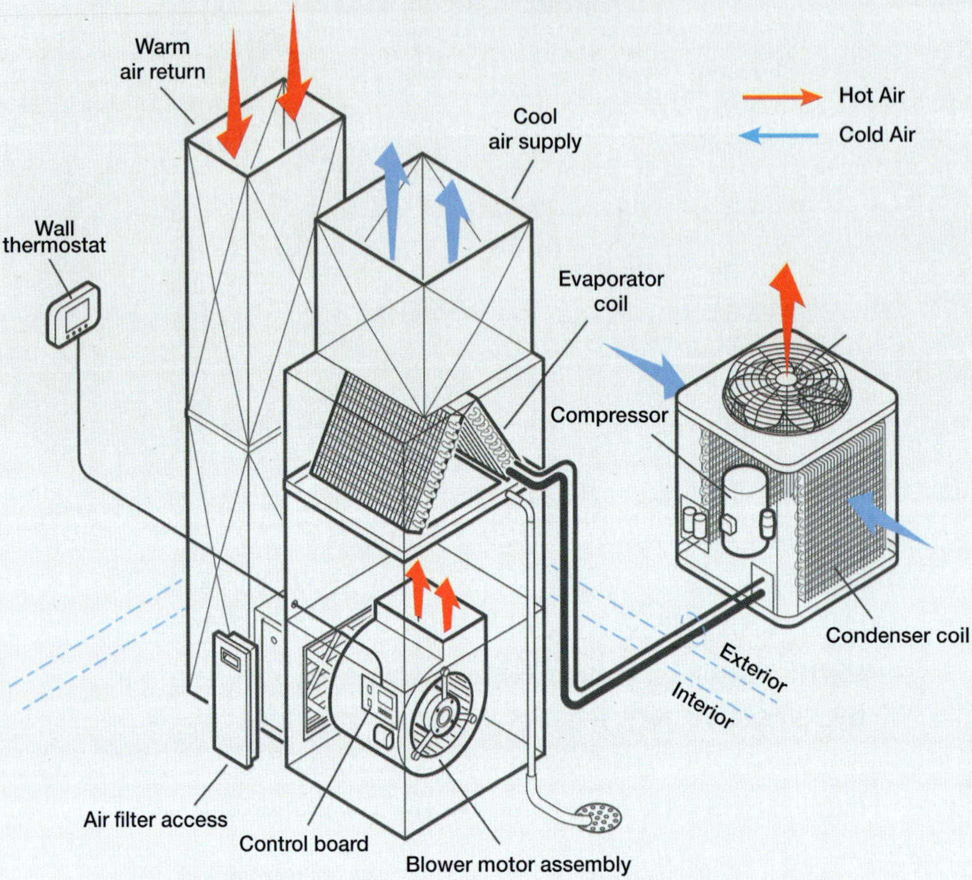

Forced air cooling systems use compressors to move refrigerant around and increase its pressure. The evaporator coil changes the refrigerant into a gas. The condenser coil changes it back into a liquid.

Other buildings have central cooling systems. A central HVAC system has tubes stretching around a building. These are called ducts. They help air move between rooms. The cooled air transfers through the ducts directly to each room. A controller called a thermostat allows people to change the temperature of the building.

There are two main types of heaters. One uses a part called a furnace to heat air. It burns fuel, which creates heat. Air travels into the furnace. It absorbs the heat. The hot air is then pumped around a building's ducts.

The other type of heater uses a part called a boiler to heat water. Boilers hold water. They burn fuel. This heats the water. The steam from the hot water or the water itself is then pumped around a building through pipes. The hot air or water warms the building.

Air filters should be replaced at least once a year.

WORKING WITH AIR QUALITY

HVAC workers also work on systems that clean indoor air. HVAC systems use filters to clean the air. Filters trap dust, pollen, and other tiny particles. Workers replace dirty filters. They make sure the air flows freely through HVAC systems.

Some HVAC workers install and fix ventilation systems. These systems bring fresh outdoor air inside. They remove stale indoor air.

Good ventilation keeps the air healthy. It reduces the spread of germs. It also prevents bad smells. By keeping the air flowing, HVAC workers help protect people's health.

INSTALLING AND REPAIRING

HVAC workers install new heating and cooling systems. An HVAC worker begins by measuring the space for a new system. Then they set up the new equipment. They connect the system's pipes and wires. Then they test the new system. They make sure it works properly. They also explain how it works to the homeowner or business owner.

HVAC workers also fix heating and cooling systems. People call when there is a problem. HVAC workers inspect the systems. They find the problems. They create a plan to fix the systems. Sometimes they repair motors. Other times they fix refrigerant leaks. They get systems working again.

Keeping Flowers Cool

Flower shops must keep their flowers at the right temperature to keep the plants bright and fresh. Flowers need the right amount of moisture in the air, too. HVAC workers make sure the air is just right. This keeps flowers looking their best.

Jarvis K. is an HVAC worker in Alabama. Repairing broken systems is one of his favorite parts of the job. He says:

When you go in somewhere, and everybody is hot and sweating . . . and you get that air conditioner going . . . It's a beautiful feeling.[4]

HVAC workers also perform maintenance. They inspect systems. They clean dirty pieces. They replace worn-out parts. They might find small problems. HVAC workers fix them before they become big problems. This helps systems last longer and work better.

SPECIAL HVAC JOBS

Some HVAC technicians work on large refrigeration systems. Grocery stores, restaurants, and hotels use large refrigeration systems. These systems keep food cold and safe to eat.

Other HVAC workers install and fix special heating and cooling systems. These might include radiant heating systems. These systems warm floors or walls.

WORKPLACES

HVAC workers can work in many different places. They may work on systems in homes. Others work in offices or shopping centers. HVAC workers are also needed in schools, hospitals, and factories.

HVAC workers often travel from place to place during the day. One job might be in a house. The next job could be in a large building. This variety makes the job

Hydronic radiant systems work by running heated water through tubes under the floor.

interesting and different every day. David Johnson is an HVAC technician. He says:

> *Being an HVAC technician is a rewarding career that keeps me on my toes. Every day brings new challenges and opportunities to solve problems. I love the hands-on nature of the work and the satisfaction of fixing things.*[5]

CHAPTER TWO

WHAT TRAINING DO HVAC TECHNICIANS NEED?

Most employers require HVAC workers to have high school diplomas. High school is where people learn many of the skills they need to succeed as HVAC workers. HVAC workers must have strong math skills. They use math to find out how much electricity a system needs. They must calculate how much refrigerant systems need. They measure how big systems should be to cool or heat a building.

In addition to having technical skills, workers must be strong enough to move heavy HVAC parts.

Science classes are also useful. Physics classes teach students about gases. Students learn about electricity. HVAC workers need to know how gases and electricity work.

HVAC workers also need technical skills. They must know how to use HVAC tools. They must be able to safely handle chemicals such as refrigerants. HVAC workers must be able to read **blueprints** to install new systems. They must understand electrical wiring and parts. HVAC workers can get these skills from vocational classes.

Some high schools offer vocational classes. These classes prepare students for trade careers. These are hands-on skilled jobs. They include plumbing, construction, and HVAC work. These classes help

Vocational classes are sometimes called shop classes.

prepare students for the next step of their career training.

TECHNICAL TRAINING

After high school, people interested in entering HVAC careers can attend HVAC training programs. Some go to trade schools. Trade schools often have HVAC technician programs. These programs

In addition to teaching students to repair HVAC systems, trade schools might teach students to fix basic wiring.

teach students how to fix and install heating and cooling systems. Students learn how air conditioners work. They learn how to use refrigerants safely. They practice using fans, ducts, and heaters. They also learn how to read simple building plans. Students even get hands-on practice fixing HVAC systems.

Trade school programs are short. Most take between 6 months and 2 years.

When a student finishes, they earn an HVAC certificate. This shows employers that they know how to work with HVAC systems.

Some students enroll in HVAC technician programs at **community colleges**. These programs take about 2 years. Students learn how to design heating and cooling systems. They learn to work with specialized HVAC systems. When a student completes the program, they earn an associate degree. Having a degree can help technicians get better jobs.

LEARNING ON THE JOB

Some people learn HVAC skills during apprenticeships. An apprenticeship pairs a beginner with a skilled worker. The technician teaches their apprentice as they work. The apprentice learns while working. They earn money as they learn. Many apprentices also go to classes.

HVAC apprenticeships usually last 3 to 5 years. **Unions**, HVAC organizations, and some companies offer these programs. Most students need to finish high school first. As they learn more, they get to do more work. When the apprenticeship ends, they are ready to work on their own.

PJ completed an HVAC apprenticeship. He started with no experience. His mentor

Virtual Training

Virtual reality (VR) helps HVAC workers learn in a fun way. A student wears special VR goggles. They see a copy of a room. They can practice fixing heaters and air conditioners without using real tools. This keeps them safe while they learn.

Many apprenticeship programs include more than 8,000 hours of on-the-job training.

helped him learn the skills he needed. He says, "Ever since day one, he took the time to teach me and made sure I understood how to do the things we needed to do. It made for some long days at the start but paid off in the long run with me understanding how things worked or why we needed to do things a certain way.

As time went on, I was able to get better, faster, and we were able to grow and learn together."[6]

EARNING CERTIFICATIONS

HVAC workers can earn certifications. These show that an HVAC worker can perform certain tasks. Some certifications are required by the government. Others show employers that HVAC workers have special skills.

The US Environmental Protection Agency (EPA) is part of the government. It protects the environment. It requires that anyone who uses refrigerants be certified. This is because refrigerant chemicals can be dangerous to the environment. HVAC workers must know how to properly

The EPA is headquartered in Washington, DC.

use refrigerants. Each worker takes a test to earn the EPA 608 certification.

Many states require HVAC workers to have licenses. To get a license, an HVAC technician must pass a test and have work experience. But not all states require this. For example, Texas HVAC workers must have licenses. They also need at least 4 years of experience. In Colorado, HVAC workers do not need licenses.

HVAC systems generally last between 10 and 15 years.

HVAC workers should check the rules in their states.

ONGOING TRAINING

Heating and cooling systems keep changing. HVAC workers need to keep learning. They can take classes to learn about new machines. They learn new ways to fix HVAC systems. Some workers earn certifications for new skills. This helps them find jobs more easily. But continued learning isn't always optional. In some states, HVAC workers must take 8 hours of classes each year to keep their licenses.

HVAC workers can also join professional organizations. These groups teach technicians about new systems and ideas. They also share news about the career field. Members can meet with other HVAC workers. They can get to know other people in their industry.

CHAPTER THREE

WHAT IS LIFE LIKE AS AN HVAC TECHNICIAN?

Most HVAC technicians start their days early. They often begin by looking at their job list for the day. They read notes from customers. They pack their tools and parts. Then they drive to their first job.

Each day is different. Some days, HVAC technicians stay in one place. Other days, they go to many homes or buildings. One day, a technician may put in a new system. Another day, they may check or fix

Driving to clients' houses is often part of an HVAC worker's responsibilities.

HVAC workers might need to work in uncomfortable spaces.

a system. They may also clean parts or put in new ducts and wires.

David Johnson enjoys working on different projects. He says, “I enjoy the variety—one day I might be on a rooftop, the next in a crawlspace. It keeps things interesting.” Johnson also likes helping his customers. "There's nothing quite like the feeling of **diagnosing** a tricky problem and getting a system up and running again," he says.[7]

HVAC workers use many tools. They often use screwdrivers, pliers, and wrenches. They use these tools to find problems with a customer's HVAC unit. Then they come up with a way to fix the system.

Johnson likes problem solving. He says, "I love putting on my detective hat and diving into a tricky HVAC issue. It's like solving a real-life puzzle every day. Sometimes I'm faced with a unit that's making weird noises or not cooling right. That's when my problem-solving skills really shine. I've got to think on my feet and use all my know-how to figure out what's wrong. It might be a faulty compressor or a clogged filter. Whatever it is, I'm on the case! The feeling when I crack the code and get that system humming again? Pure gold."[8]

After an HVAC worker finishes a job, they explain to the customer what they did. They show the customer how to use their system. At the end of the day, they write notes and clean tools. They get ready for the next day.

HOURS AND SCHEDULES

Most HVAC workers work full time. This means they work about 40 hours per week. Some work evenings or on weekends. They may work overtime during busy

HVAC workers must have customer service skills.

heating and cooling seasons. This includes heat waves and very cool periods.

Many HVAC companies have workers on call. These workers answer emergency calls from customers. An emergency might happen when a system stops working during extreme heat or cold. Other emergencies include gas leaks, electrical problems, strange noises, or burning smells.

Emergency calls can come in at any time of day or night.

WORK ENVIRONMENT

HVAC technicians work in many different places. They work in homes, offices, hospitals, and other buildings. They must travel to each jobsite.

Soft Skills

HVAC workers must have soft skills. Soft skills are people skills. They help a person get along with others. HVAC workers must be good communicators. They need to talk to customers and coworkers. They must be able to explain problems. They also need to be able to suggest solutions. HVAC workers must also manage their time well. They need to show up at jobsites on time. A single worker will often juggle multiple customers in a day.

Most HVAC work is indoors. Technicians might need to work in cramped spaces such as attics or crawl spaces. They also might have to work in awkward positions. They might need to kneel, bend, or stretch overhead to reach the area they must repair. This makes the job physically demanding. The space might also be uncomfortable if the heat or air conditioning is not working.

HVAC workers occasionally have to work outdoors. They might need to repair pieces of HVAC systems that are outside. They may have to work in the hot sun, heavy rain, or very cold temperatures.

RISKS AND DANGERS

HVAC work can be dangerous. Workers lift heavy machines. Hot pipes can burn skin.

Safety gear is often called personal protective equipment, or PPE.

Sharp metal can cut workers. Chemicals can hurt the skin or lungs. Wires can give electric shocks. To stay safe, HVAC workers learn safety rules. These steps help keep them safe.

HVAC workers also protect themselves with safety gear. Gloves protect their hands. Safety glasses protect their eyes. Masks protect workers from getting dust and mold in their lungs. On building sites, workers wear hard hats. This protects them from falling debris.

CHAPTER FOUR

WHAT IS THE FUTURE FOR HVAC TECHNICIANS?

The future for HVAC workers looks bright. Workers will be needed to put in new heating and cooling systems. They will also be needed to fix and maintain old systems. Workers who learn about new equipment and tools will have many opportunities.

The Bureau of Labor Statistics (BLS) is a US agency. It keeps track of information about different jobs. That includes how

In 2024, the median annual salary for an HVAC worker was $59,810.

many people are in each career field. In 2024, the BLS reported that there were about 425,200 jobs for HVAC technicians. This number is growing. In 2024, the BLS predicted that the number of HVAC technician jobs in the United States will

Almost 90 percent of buildings in the United States have HVAC systems. Many workers are needed to service these systems.

grow by about 8 percent from 2024 to 2034. This growth is faster than the average for all jobs. More workers will be needed in the next few years. The BLS predicts there will be 459,700 HVAC jobs by 2034.

Each year, many new HVAC workers will be needed. The BLS estimates there will be about 40,100 open HVAC jobs each year over the next 10 years. Some workers will retire or change jobs. New workers will have to take their places.

FUTURE NEEDS

In the future, HVAC workers will be needed in many places. One important area is new construction. New homes and buildings need heating and cooling systems. HVAC workers will help put these systems in.

In 2026, there were nearly 4,000 data centers in the United States.

People also want to save energy and keep the air clean. Many buildings will need better heating and cooling systems. HVAC workers will be needed to fix, change, and improve these systems.

HVAC workers are also needed to work in data centers. These are places that run and train artificial intelligence (AI) technology. This is technology that can do complex tasks. It can sort data. It can write and create images. It can even learn.

Data centers use a lot of electricity. They also get very hot. They need HVAC workers to cool the centers down. This keeps the machines working smoothly.

SMART TECHNOLOGY

Smart technology is changing heating and cooling. Smart HVAC systems use tiny **sensors** and computers. They monitor the air and change the temperature when needed. Smart systems can also tell when something is wrong. They send alerts to owners.

Many smart HVAC systems use the internet. People can use phones or tablets to change their houses' temperature. They can turn their HVAC systems on and off remotely. These smart systems help buildings stay comfortable while saving energy.

Some HVAC systems use AI. AI watches how a system works. It looks for signs of trouble. The system can send a message to an owner when a part needs to be replaced. This helps prevent big problems.

HVAC workers must learn to use smart technology as it develops. They will need to know how smart systems work to fix problems. They will need to use apps to check for needed repairs and parts. Technicians who can work with smart technology will have more job opportunities.

USING LESS ENERGY

Energy costs are rising. People also want to help the Earth. They look for ways to

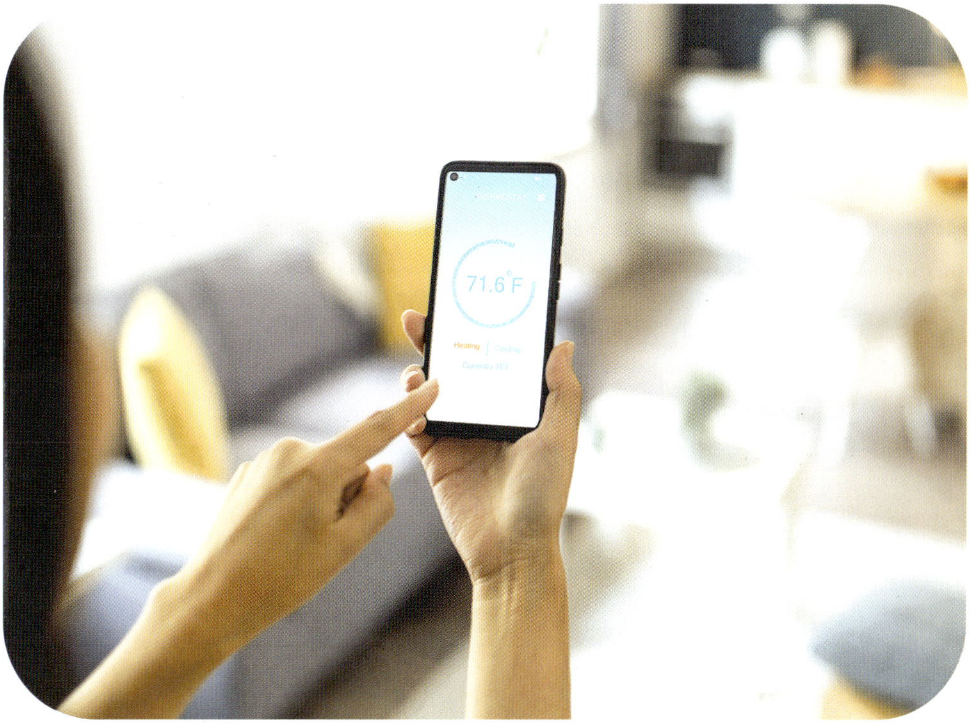

Smart HVAC systems can save money by reducing heating or cooling when residents are away from their homes.

save energy. One way to save energy is to use energy-efficient HVAC systems. These systems use less energy than traditional HVAC systems. But they still keep buildings comfortable.

Ductless systems do not use ducts. They send warm or cool air right into each room. This helps save energy because no air is lost inside the ducts. HVAC workers who can install and repair these systems will be needed.

Geothermal systems use heat from the ground. A few feet underground, Earth's temperature stays almost the same all year. Geothermal systems use special pipes buried underground. In winter, the pipes pull heat from the ground to warm homes. In summer, the pipes move heat from homes back into the ground to keep houses cool.

New Eco-Friendly Refrigerants

Some old refrigerants are harmful to Earth's **atmosphere**. But people are creating new refrigerants that are eco-friendly. These new refrigerants are better for Earth's atmosphere. Many new HVAC systems use these safer gases. HVAC workers should know how to work with them.

Other systems use energy from the sun. Solar panels can generate electricity to power HVAC systems. As solar power technology improves, more buildings may use it to power their HVAC systems. Workers who know how to install and fix these systems will be needed.

Benjamin Ficklin teaches air conditioning technology to students at San Jacinto College in Texas. He encourages students to think about entering HVAC careers. He explains that there are a lot of job openings for skilled HVAC workers. These jobs also pay well. "It's a career that truly matters," says Ficklin. "HVAC is a trade where effort leads directly to success, and every day brings a chance to learn something new."[9]

GLOSSARY

atmosphere

the layer of gas above Earth's surface

blueprints

detailed drawings that show how to build something

community colleges

schools that offer educational programs, often 2-year programs and certificates, in specific areas of study

diagnosing

identifying or determining

geothermal

related to the heat that comes from inside the Earth

inspected

looked closely at something

maintenance

work done to keep something working well

sensors

devices that notice specific things and relay that information to others

unions

groups of people, especially those in the same fields, with common goals

SOURCE NOTES

INTRODUCTION: KEEPING COOL IN A HEAT WAVE

1. Quoted in Madeleine Wright, "HVAC Technicians Staying Busy amid Heat Wave in Philadelphia Region," *CBS News*, July 29, 2025. www.cbsnews.com.

2. Quoted in Wright, "HVAC Technicians Staying Busy amid Heat Wave."

3. Quoted in Wright, "HVAC Technicians Staying Busy amid Heat Wave."

CHAPTER ONE: WHAT DOES AN HVAC TECHNICIAN DO?

4. Quoted in "Four Things HVAC-R Techs Love About Their Jobs," *Fortis Colleges and Institutes*, September 1, 2021. www.fortis.edu

5. David Johnson, "What Do You Enjoy About Being an HVAC Technician? The Coolest Job You've Never Considered," *HVAC Service Bellevue*, August 13, 2025. https://hvacservicebellevue.com.

CHAPTER TWO: WHAT TRAINING DO HVAC TECHNICIANS NEED?

6. Quoted in "Trane Accreditation," *Logan Services*, n.d. www.logan-inc.com.

CHAPTER THREE: WHAT IS LIFE LIKE AS AN HVAC TECHNICIAN?

7. Johnson, "What Do You Enjoy About Being an HVAC Technician?"

8. Johnson, "What Do You Enjoy About Being an HVAC Technician?"

CHAPTER FOUR: WHAT IS THE FUTURE FOR HVAC TECHNICIANS?

9. Quoted in Dax Stokes, "HVAC Gators: Powering the Future," *San Jacinto Times*, November 7, 2025. https://sanjactimes.com.

FOR FURTHER RESEARCH

BOOKS

Cynthia Kennedy Henzel, *Vocational Careers in Construction*. BrightPoint Press, 2026.

Stuart A. Kallen, *Exploring Jobs in the Skilled Trades*. ReferencePoint Press, 2023.

Ashley Kuehl, *Become a Construction Technician: Carpentry, Plumbing & More*. Abdo Publishing, 2025.

INTERNET SOURCES

"Careers Corner: A Day in the Life of an HVAC Technician," *Lee Company*, July 9, 2025. www.leecompany.com.

"How To Become an HVAC Technician," *Indeed*, December 11, 2025. www.indeed.com.

"What Does an HVAC Technician Do?" *Career Explorer*, n.d. www.careerexplorer.com.

WEBSITES

Air Conditioning Contractors of America

www.acca.org

The Air Conditioning Contractors of America is a nonprofit association for professionals who install and maintain HVAC systems. Its website has links to educational resources for HVAC technicians.

American Society of Heating, Refrigerating and Air-Conditioning Engineers

www.ashrae.org

The American Society of Heating, Refrigerating and Air-Conditioning Engineers is an international society of HVAC professionals. The organization has resources for young people who are interested in HVAC careers.

SkillsUSA

www.skillsusa.org

SkillsUSA is a national nonprofit organization for students preparing for careers in technical, skilled, and service occupations. The organization provides students with scholarships and resources to further their careers.

INDEX

IMAGE CREDITS

Cover: © spates/iStockphoto
5: © Hryshchyshen Serhii/Shutterstock Images
7: © DC Studio/Shutterstock Images
8: © AT Production/Shutterstock Images
11: © DC Studio/Shutterstock Images
12: © Vics Photos/Shutterstock Images
15: © VlJ/iStockphoto
17: © MyrKu/iStockphoto
18: © befehr/iStockphoto
20: © Studio Romantic/Shutterstock Images
25: © romaset/iStockphoto
27: © ftwitty/iStockphoto
29: © andresr/iStockphoto
30: © Poguz.P/Shutterstock Images
33: © Alpa Prod/Shutterstock Images
35: © Erik Cox Photography/Shutterstock Images
36: © sturti/iStockphoto
39: © Andrey_Popov/Shutterstock Images
40: © Global_Pics/iStockphoto
43: © Spiderstock/iStockphoto
46: © CandyRetriever/Shutterstock Images
49: © Master1305/Shutterstock Images
50: © PeopleImages/Shutterstock Images
52: © Snehit Photo/Shutterstock Images
55: © SrdjanPav/iStockphoto

ABOUT THE AUTHOR

Carla Mooney is a graduate of the University of Pennsylvania. She is the author of many books for young people.